NVQs
and how to get them
HAZEL DAKERS

KOGAN
PAGE

With thanks to the colleagues,
family and other friends who stood by me during 1995.

Kogan Page Limited
120 Pentonville Road
London N1 9JN

© Hazel Dakers, 1996

British Library Cataloguing in Publication Data

A CIP record for this book is available from the British Library.

ISBN 0 7494 1976 8

Typeset by Northern Phototypesetting Co. Ltd, Bolton
Printed and bound in Great Britain by Biddles Ltd, Guildford and King's Lynn

CONTENTS

FOREWORD

One of the most exciting developments in the world of learning in recent years has been the acceptance of the concept of competence as being the right basis for the UK's National Vocational Qualification (NVQ) system. In this context, competence can be defined as the ability to apply knowledge, understanding and skills in order to do a job to the required standard. This includes solving problems and meeting the changing demands of the workplace.

This development has not been without its own set of problems. Some educationalists, brought up on a system of norm-referenced examinations, still find it difficult to understand what is in effect a criterion-referenced system. Not surprisingly, many awarding bodies have been ambiguous at moving over from their own tried and tested examinations to the new regime. In spite of the recent award of the one millionth NVQ (December 1995), take up of NVQs by employees and individuals has been slower than some would have wished – though we have to remember that it took the Germans several decades to put their systems in place.

However, make no mistake, the NVQ/SVQ system is here to stay and it has the support of all the main political parties, employer bodies and the trade unions. The CBI has taken the view that the skills revolution on which the UK has embarked, and which is so essential to our future competitiveness and economic well-being, can only be sustained if individuals are empowered to play a full role.

NVQs and SVQs are the main currency of both the skills revolution and of the lifetime national education and training targets. For anyone looking to maximize their prospects for employment in an increasingly competitive world, the acquisition of NVQs provides the way forward.

I welcome this guide as an important contribution to demystifying what NVQs are all about and explaining how you can go out and, with the help of your employer and others, acquire one. It fills a gap in existing provision and will bring home to all concerned why NVQs are going to play such a large part in all our futures.

Tony Webb
Director of Education and Training
CBI

INTRODUCTION

'Which is the book about NVQs we should all have on our library shelves?' I was asked at a meeting of senior public librarians. My response was that I should like to write it. So here it is.

If you have heard that an NVQ would be a good way to further your career and you wonder how and why, this is a straightforward explanation of NVQs and how to get them. The subject is usually, though quite unnecessarily, veiled in mystery. NVQs are for everyone and so everyone should be able to find out easily how to acquire them. This book sets out to help you do just that.

Books abound on the theory and concepts of competence, work-based learning, functional analysis and the different means of assessment. I touch on these issues but only to the extent that you need to understand them to get an NVQ.

As a driver I know I have to put petrol in my car, but I make no attempt to understand its construction or maintenance needs. I leave those things to the manufacturer and the service engineer. Similarly, I assume that the potential NVQ candidate will need to feel assured as to the quality of the qualification. The candidate needs to operate within the system in the same way as I need to operate my car.

I assure any Scottish readers that I am fully aware of the existence of SVQs. To simplify the book I have only referred to NVQs but in nearly every respect they are the same. Relevant Scottish abbreviations and sources of further information have been included.

By the end of this book I hope you will feel that the NVQ system is a well thought out and useful one. I hope you will be excited at the prospect of embarking on an NVQ, and that you will have enjoyed reading about how to get it.

© REATEA

Acknowledgements

I would like to thank the Lead Bodies and ITOs and their artists who have permitted the use of illustrations in this book. They are: The Biscuit, Cake, Chocolate and Confectionery Alliance (BCCCA) and Barry Jackson, pages 18 and 73; BLC, The Leather Technology Centre, pages 34 and 77; Management Charter Initiative (MCI), pages 4, 41 and 67; The Residential Estate Agency Training and Education Association (REATEA), page vi; and Periodicals Training Council (PTC), pages 2, 9, 15, 23, 37 and 81. The example of an element used throughout Chapter 8 is included with the kind permission of the Administration Lead Body.

I am very grateful for the time given up by my volunteer readers, Justin Arundale, Miriam Bennett, Kate and Peter Evans, Stephen Hunt, Eleanor von Schweinitz and David Whitaker, who helped me develop the published version with their comments on the original draft. Thank you also to Brenda Birney and Chris Dakers for helping me to check the proofs. Dolores Black at Kogan Page encouraged me to write on and patiently answered my very basic questions concerning publication.

My son Andrew has resolved most of my IT and design problems in preparing the drafts and set me the additional challenge of teaching myself a new word processing program at the same time as writing the book!

1. WHAT IS AN NVQ?

- ⇨ Background
- ⇨ Definition
- ⇨ What's special about NVQs?
- ⇨ Competent and not yet competent
- ⇨ More useful facts about NVQs

⇨ Background

Is there a National Vocational Qualification (NVQ) for your kind of work? Almost certainly there is or there will be very soon. More than 160 sets of National Vocational Qualifications (NVQs) are being developed to cover nearly every kind of work that people do in Great Britain. The 160 sets are divided into 11 very broad groups. NVQs are developed at five levels ranging from the quite straightforward at level 1 to the very complex at level 5. You will find the 160 sets of NVQs listed on p.87 at the back of this book and the detail of the levels explained on p.68.

This is a very new qualifications system. The ideas for it were first put forward in the mid-1980s and some of the qualifications are still being developed. The main reason for devising a new system was that as a country we were doing very badly compared with our economic rivals. The government noticed that our successful competitors had more highly qualified workforces in most occupations. It therefore decided that our future economic success probably depended upon better training and qualifications.

The government also discovered that in Great Britain we had a great variety of different kinds of qualification. Consequently employers looking for staff were unable to work out which applicants had the qualifications most suited to the job vacancy. So the government decided to draw up the NVQ Framework of 11 broad groups of NVQs at five levels within which all NVQs are placed. This NVQ Framework provides a basis to link with other national and international qualifications.

⇨ Definition

If you have a National Vocational Qualification (NVQ) it shows that you can do the work for which it has been awarded and do it to the *national standard*. This means that you are *competent* in this kind of work. For this reason NVQs are described as *competence-based qualifications*.

An NVQ *reflects* a typical kind of *job*. It will not be exactly the same as your particular job but it will be very much the same as a group of similar jobs.

The *best* place to be *checked* to see whether you have reached the standard of an NVQ, or a part of one, is *at work*. Only at work can it be seen that you carry out your job competently – to the national standard.

You may have to do some *training* before you are assessed. Some of this training may be away from your job, or you may find you do all of it at work.

DEFINITION

- An NVQ is a competence-based qualification
- An NVQ reflects the needs of the workplace
- An NVQ is best assessed in the workplace
- Achievement of an NVQ will often require training

⇨ What's special about NVQs?

You will read a full example of an element of an NVQ in Chapter 8. Here, we will look at some of the special features of NVQs so that you can begin to see what makes them different from other qualifications.

NVQs state very clearly what has been done to carry out an activity competently. These results are listed in a very straightforward way. The list is called the Performance Criteria (p.48).

NVQs check whether you can carry out these Performance Criteria in a variety of different contexts. These contexts are called Range (p.49). If you have an NVQ to show that you work competently it will also show that you are competent in a whole lot of different situations.

NVQs show what you can do. However, in order to *do* it is often necessary also to *know*. This deeper understanding of what you are doing is called Underpinning Knowledge and Understanding (p.49).

If you have an NVQ to show that you are competent according to our

national occupational standards it will show your abilities in three
directions:

1. You will be able to carry out your work in most usual situations.
2. You will be able to carry out your work in a variety of different sit-
    uations.
3. You will be able to carry out your work with understanding.

SPECIAL FEATURES OF NVQs

- NVQ elements contain Performance Criteria (results of actions taken)
- NVQ elements contain Range (contexts)
- NVQ elements contain Underpinning Knowledge and Understanding (UKU) (theory, principles)

⇨ **Competent and not yet competent**

Thinking of school exam grades, do you realize that with our 'Cs', 'Ds', 'Es' and 'Fs' we passed well, quite well, not that well and only just! Which of those grades shows that our abilities are of a good enough standard to do a job properly?

When our new qualifications were being devised it was decided to look at them in a different way. It seemed more sensible to first decide what are the criteria necessary to carry out a given job competently and then measure people against those criteria. In this way the standard would be even from year to year. This is called *criterion-referencing*.

National Vocational Qualifications are criterion-referenced. If you take NVQs you either do or do not match up to the standard or criteria. If you do match up you are assessed as *competent*. If you do not match up to the criteria you are assessed as *not yet competent*. You cannot be excellently competent, very competent, very nearly competent or half competent. Competence exists or does not yet exist!

You will already be used to this attitude if you have taken swimming certificates as a child, or the driving test. You are either safe to be let loose or you are not yet safe and can try the test again. No examiner is going to pass you for being half safe, I hope.

⇨ **More useful facts about NVQs**

NVQs cover approximately 160 areas of work. The NVQ Framework
links NVQs at all five levels, of which level 1 is the lowest level of difficulty. (Chapter 11 tells you more about levels and there is a list of occupational areas on p.87.)

This should make it easier, once you are in the NVQ system, to move
jobs. You will be able to show that what you have learned in one job is
valuable in another. You can enter the system at any point you have
agreed with your assessor. In other words, to take a level 3 there is no
need first to achieve levels 1 and 2. You can only register for the level at
which you are working in your job. There is a description of NVQ levels
on page 68. As you will see, they go from quite junior to very senior
jobs.

You can work through the units which make up an NVQ at your own
pace. You do not have to spend a particular period studying before you
are assessed. Your assessor will judge the evidence of what you can *do*
– not what you have been *taught*.

THE NVQ SYSTEM

- The NVQ Framework covers approximately
  160 occupational areas
- The NVQ Framework covers 5 levels
- The NVQ system may be entered at any level
- NVQs are achieved by demonstrating work
  carried out to the national standard

PROGRESS LIST

This progress list is here to remind you what you will learn about NVQs in this book and what stage you have reached so far.

☑ What is an NVQ?

❑ Why take an NVQ?

❑ How to become an NVQ candidate

❑ What is an assessment centre?

❑ What does the assessor do?

❑ What does the candidate do?

❑ What makes up an NVQ?

❑ What makes up an element?

❑ A portfolio?

❑ What next?

❑ The NVQ framework

❑ Persuading your boss about NVQs

Where to find out more
Abbreviations and jargon

Now you know what an NVQ is. Next you are going to look at the reasons why you may wish to register for an NVQ.

2. WHY TAKE AN NVQ?

⇨ Reasons

⇨ National standard of comptence

⇨ Not the same as a course

⇨ No barriers to entry

⇨ Flexibility and transferability

⇨ NVQs and academic qualifications

⇨ Reasons

I expect you will be thinking of taking an NVQ for one of several reasons.

1. You are considering it because it is the new kind of qualification.
2. You want to prove to yourself and others just how able you are.
3. You think it will help you to progress in your career.

⇨ **National standard of competence**

NVQs may only be achieved through the demonstration of skills. Getting your NVQ will show that you have proved your abilities to the national standard. The national occupational standards express the way in which work may best be carried out now. If you work to those standards you are considered competent now. In terms of work, a qualification which proves that you can do your job competently must be a very valuable possession.

⇨ **Not the same as a course**

Have you noticed, the word 'course' has not yet been mentioned? NVQs are about far more than courses. After all, you can sit through hours, days, weeks or even years of a course and yet no one has any means of knowing what you have gained from it. And there is no proof that you can put the learning into practice. *NVQs show that you can do as well as know.*

It may be that to assist you with taking your NVQ you may take a course or two. A course may help you to fill in some gaps on matters of which you have only learned a little on the job. In particular, courses may help you to acquire the Underpinning Knowledge and Understanding (UKU) – theory and principles – without which it is unlikely you will be competent (see p.49). People need to know *why* they are doing things to do them well and *what* to do when things go wrong.

An NVQ is not proof that you can repeat what you learned on a course. An NVQ is proof that your skills match the national standard of work performance.

NOT THE SAME AS A COURSE

An NVQ measures:
- Your ability to do and know
- Your underpinning knowledge and understanding
- Your formal and informal training
- Your formal or informal testing

⇨ No barriers to entry

You do not need any other formal qualification to allow you to work towards your NVQ. Nor do you need the level of NVQ below that which you now want to acquire. What you do need is to establish, usually with the help of your employer, which NVQ at what level best corresponds with the job you do. You can only be assessed for what you actually do.

You can put evidence towards your NVQ which you collected from working temporarily, part-time, full-time or voluntarily. People have obtained them through experimental projects based on unpaid work in the home.

Neither language nor disability nor age can pose a barrier to entry provided that the candidate is able to carry out the work to the national standard.

Training to the national standard is what NVQs are all about. You may learn in many ways: by being shown how to carry something out by a colleague or supervisor, by reading a book, by watching a video or by computer-assisted training. As far as NVQs are concerned, it does not matter how you acquired your skills as long as they are of the national standard.

NO BARRIERS TO NVQ ENTRY

- No prior qualification needed
- Language need not stop you
- Disability need be no barrier
- Age need not prevent you becoming an NVQ candidate

⇨ Flexibility and transferability

NVQs make your skills more transferable. That is, a skill you have acquired in one place through one activity can be taken with you to a different situation. You may not do book-keeping in your current job but you may do it as treasurer of your local football team or playgroup. Evidence from this hobby counts towards the NVQ (if it is an NVQ that includes some book-keeping). In turn the NVQ acts as proof that you can do book-keeping competently when you next apply for a job.

NVQs also demonstrate flexibility in using your skills. During your assessment you will exhibit your abilities in applications different from those with which you most usually work. You will demonstrate that you are flexible enough to adapt what is fundamentally the same activity working in a different context.

As time goes on it looks as though NVQs will have a future both as national and international currency for employment.

THE FLEXIBILITY AND TRANSFERABILITY OF NVQs

- Skills may be taken from one situation to another
- People are able to apply skills in different situations
- Value overseas

⇨ NVQs and academic qualifications

So, what is the special difference between NVQs and traditional qualifications?

Academic qualifications, GCSEs, A levels, degrees and so on, are awarded through the acquisition of a body of knowledge selected by an examination board, a group of teachers or lecturers. This knowledge is what these education providers consider to be a useful collection of learning. If you take one of these qualifications the success of your learning is tested either by assignment or by examination, or both. The practical examinations in subjects such as science, art and geography are simulated exercises designed to test learning but do not set out to prove capability for work. The learning is usually done in a prescribed way by following a course.

If you are awarded an NVQ this will be because you have achieved the outcomes (results of activities) identified as necessary to carry out an occupation. Many forms of evidence may be used to show that these outcomes have been reached and it does not matter how you have achieved them.

DIFFERENCES BETWEEN NVQs AND ACADEMIC QUALIFICATIONS

NVQs:
- Match nationally identified needs for work
- Make use of many forms of evidence and are assessed in many ways

Academic qualifications:
- Are based on topics selected by course providers
- Are tested by assignment and/or exam

SELF ASSESSMENT CHECKLIST

Please complete this self-assessment checklist to help decide if an NVQ might be right for you. Do you want:

	Yes	No
To be qualified as competent at your work?	☐	☐
To take a qualification without having to take a course?	☐	☐
To have an opportunity to qualify whoever you are, no matter what your previous educational experience?	☐	☐
To have a qualification which proves your skills are transferable and towards which skills acquired anywhere may count?	☐	☐
To qualify to the national standards needed in your work rather than to those of providers of education and training?	☐	☐

If you answered 'Yes' to most of these questions, move on to the next chapter!

3. HOW TO BECOME AN NVQ CANDIDATE

⇨ Find an approved assessment centre

⇨ Awarding bodies

⇨ Initial assessment

⇨ Register for your NVQ

⇨ Use the services of the assessment centre

⇨ Find an approved assessment centre

There are several places to find out about a convenient approved assessment centre:

1. Your employer
2. Your local TEC (Training and Enterprise Council)
3. The awarding body for NVQs in your field

4. The Lead Body or ITO (Industry Training Organization) for your job
5. Your public library
6. Your local careers office.

You may think it is difficult to find out through either the awarding body or the Lead Body or ITO because you do not know which yours is. NCVQ (the National Council for Vocational Qualifications) will be able to help you identify the right one (see 'Where to find out more' on p.82).

Candidates all have to register with an assessment centre. This will have been approved for the particular NVQ the candidate wishes to take.

Different assessment centres will offer different services to candidates. If you live or work in an area where there is a choice of assessment centres for your NVQ, find out what each one has to offer.

⇨ Awarding bodies

Some NVQs may be obtained from several different awarding bodies. The NVQ is worth exactly the same but you may be more used to the way one awarding body goes about its work than another. You could therefore find several assessment centres in your area approved for the same NVQ by different awarding bodies.

© PTC

There are a great many awarding bodies. Amongst the best known are BTEC (Business and Technology Education Council), CGLI (City and Guilds of London Institute) and RSA (Royal Society of Arts) Examination Board. In certain occupations, an awarding body has been chosen for its specialism within the particular field. All have to work to the same rules laid down by NCVQ (the National Council for Vocational Qualifications).

⇨ Initial assessment

As you already know, there is no pre-entry requirement restricting the level at which you may enter the NVQ system. However, your work, upon which evidence you will be assessed, must include the activities to be assessed.

An initial assessment is essential to find the correct starting point. This might be a checklist you skim through on your own or with one of the centre staff. It might very well be carried out as an informal chat. If you are having a preliminary look for yourself, look at the contents of each unit of the qualifications in detail and then see which units go to make up which level of qualification. For some very popular NVQs, special booklets called 'Skillscans' have been published to help you in this initial assessment. You know what your work is so you will have a very good idea of the NVQ level which is suitable for you.

At this point it is also likely that some gaps will be identified in your skills. Some element of planning to fill those gaps should come into play at this stage.

Those of you who have traditional qualifications already should consider this warning. You may be very highly qualified academically but that is not an automatic indication of your likely NVQ level. Your current job may not reflect the potential indicated by your academic qualification. The NVQ will be a useful further qualification which will demonstrate that not only do you *know* (which is proved by your academic qualification) but you can also *do*.

An initial assessment:

- Will help to find a starting point
- Will establish what your job includes
- Will explain why previous qualifications may be no indication of level

⇨ Register for your NVQ

This will be the first formal step you take towards getting an NVQ. When you pay your registration fee to the assessment centre, you are committing yourself to qualifying as competent. This will cost between about £15 and £40 depending on the level and size of the NVQ. If you are lucky your employer will be paying as part of a staff development programme.

If you are paying for yourself do check out whether the TEC (Training and Enterprise Council) in whose region you either live or work is able to give you any assistance. Each TEC has its own priorities for support. If you are paying for some training which contributes towards your NVQ, find out whether the training provider has registered it with the Inland Revenue for tax relief and therefore whether you can pay a reduced fee. If this is the case, your centre will ask you to complete form VTR1. Certificates for each unit which you are awarded are likely to cost about £5.50 each, the total depending on the level and size of the NVQ. The 'scheme book', in which an NVQ is published will usually cost about £5.

REGISTER FOR YOUR NVQ

- Registration cost about £15–£40
- Certificates cost about £5.50 per unit
- Total cost depends on level and size of NVQ
- Sources of help:
    Employer
    TEC
    Inland Revenue

YOU WANT AN NVQ FOR WHAT?

⇨ Use the services of the assessment centre

Remember that you are the customer of a training and qualifications service. This service is being offered by the centre at which you have registered. Make sure, if there are alternative centres available, that you have selected the centre of greatest benefit to you.

Most will provide courses of one sort or another designed to help you fill those training gaps identified in your initial assessment. You will almost certainly have needed to commit yourself to the cost of this training – which is likely to have assessment built into it – as a requirement of registering with the centre.

These days training is not only traditional courses. It may well include an element of 'open learning'. This is largely an independent activity which is often focused upon the resources of a library/information centre or distance learning. Use any resources offered. The responsibility is very much with you as the candidate. If your employing organization has registered as a centre you will almost certainly have the opportunity for planned training on the job. The centre will provide at least one member of staff to whom you will have access for guidance. Be guided!

The centre may well arrange group meetings of candidates for mutual support and self help. Take advantage of these. The NVQ system is intended to be tailored to the individual's needs. Make sure it is tailored to *your* needs.

Use your assessment centre to provide:

- Formal/informal gap filling training
- Traditional courses
- Open/distance learning
- Support for planned learning on the job

But responsibility remains with candidate
supported by:
    centre staff
    other candidates

CHECKLIST: ACTION PLAN TO BECOME A CANDIDATE

Use this checklist below to help you plan the steps you need to take to become an NVQ candidate.

(tick box when complete)

1. Find out what centres are convenient to you ☐

2. Compare facilities ☐

3. Compare fees ☐

4. Investigate financial help ☐

5. Select most suitable for you ☐

6. Undergo initial assessment ☐

7. Register for level advised ☐

8. Use your assessment centre ☐

4. WHAT IS AN ASSESSMENT CENTRE?

⇨ Definition

⇨ Where is an assessment centre?

⇨ For and against different types

⇨ Definition

An assessment centre is an organization rather than a physical place. In other words, an organization operating on several sites would still be one centre.

To become a centre, an organization has to comply with the rules of the awarding body. These rules are a reflection of the regulations established by NCVQ. All these regulations exist to ensure that you, the candidate, are assured quality and equivalence no matter at which centre you are registered.

Broadly speaking, your centre is expected to have certain resources, including management systems, suitably qualified and competent staff, adequate physical resources, quality and assessment procedures. As in all other aspects of NVQs you will expect to find equality of opportunity and access.

To explain this in another way, you will expect to find a well planned assessment programme with proper communication taking place between the staff involved. These staff will be qualified by the EOSC (Employment Occupational Standards Council) to carry out their duties to the national standard and they will be designated competent in the occupational area for which you are being assessed. You will expect to find efficient records and regular monitoring for quality. NCVQ expects centres to make provision for special needs. You might wish to enquire about these arrangements when you are comparing centres.

DEFINITION OF AN ASSESSMENT CENTRE

An organization which complies with NCVQ regulations regarding:

- Quality management systems
- Qualified staff
- Adequate physical resources
- Quality assurance
- Assessment services
- Equality of opportunity
- Open access

⇨ Where is an assessment centre?

If you work for a large organization and are lucky, your *employing organization* will be an approved assessment centre for the NVQ you want to take. As the evidence put towards the assessment for your NVQ will largely come from your job, a centre at your workplace is the one most likely to be tailored to the needs of your job. Equally it is far more likely that your boss will give you opportunities to widen your experience and cover all the necessary Range, if you are taking your NVQ at work. From the organization's point of view, the qualification will be seen as more closely answering its own needs.

If your employing organization is an assessment centre, it is most likely to match the training it organizes to the skills gaps which you need to fill to obtain your NVQ. An atmosphere will be more likely in which staff are expected to be constantly improving their skills. Support of many kinds will be given for self-improvement in the learning organization.

This kind of assessment centre will almost certainly be entirely financed by your employer. Your assessor might be your line manager or a member of staff from the training department.

Some employing organizations are just too small, or have too few staff of a particular occupation, for it to be worth their while becoming an assessment centre. Those who see the need for one closely linked with the workplace will sometimes join a *consortium assessment centre*. A group of organizations will cooperatively share assessment facilities. If you are being assessed through one of these centres you will have the additional interest of coming into contact with candidates and assessors from other similar organizations. Training arrangements may well be cooperative. Your assessor might still be your own line manager, but equally could come from another organization. Your employer is still almost certain to foot the bill.

Training and education providers may also become assessment centres. These could include your local college of further education, universities, independent (commercial) training organizations and TECs (Training and Enterprise Councils). These organizations have viewed assessment as an additional service which will enhance their education and training provision.

Some NVQs will be more suited than others to assessment away from the job or *simulations* (mock-ups) of work situations. For this reason some assessment centres will be approved to cover certain units of an NVQ but not a whole one. Others will provide courses designed to provide only the *Underpinning Knowledge* towards an NVQ.

In some cases, assessors no longer usually working in your field will be expected to spend regular time back on the job to retain current occupational competence. This practical experience will ensure that they can still *do* what they are assessing and are not out of date.

Some candidates will use non-work-based centres individually, paying for themselves, and others will be sponsored by their employers.

Many of the same advantages and disadvantages will apply to *independent training providers* (such as commercial training organizations and other independent training institutions) as to colleges and universities. Some will have particularly strong links with certain industries or employing organizations and their smaller size may make them more flexible in matching your needs. On the other hand their smaller size may also result in fewer physical resources. More of the staff may spend part of their time practising their occupation as well as teaching it. They may appear to have less monitoring of their training activities than a college – but remember they will have to be good to stay in business. Payment may be by you or your employer.

WHERE IS A SUITABLE ASSESSMENT CENTRE?

- At work?
- A consortium of linked organizations?
- The local FE college?
- A nearby university?
- The regional TEC?
- A specialist independent training provider?

PROGRESS LIST

This progress list reminds you of what you will learn about NVQs in this book and what stage you have reached so far.

☑ What is an NVQ

☑ Why take an NVQ?

☑ How to become an NVQ candidate

☑ What is an assessment centre?

☐ What does the assessor do?

☐ What does the candidate do?

☐ What makes up an NVQ?

☐ What makes up an element?

☐ A portfolio?

☐ What next?

☐ The NVQ framework

☐ Persuading your boss about NVQs

Where to find out more
Abbreviations and jargon

Now let's take a look at what the key people do.

ALTERNATIVE TYPES OF ASSESSMENT CENTRE

	FOR	AGAINST
Work/consortiuim	1. Fits closely with job, internal career structure	1. May seem too narrow a learning experience
	2. Employer supportive towards learner – attitudes, training	2. May not wish to be assessed by direct boss or other senior staff
	3. Assessor really understands what is being assessed as works there too	3. May feel less responsible for own development and more directed
	4. Employer pays	
FE college/university	1. Widens experience socially	1. May seem remote from workplace
	2. Widens experience of occupation	2. Mock-ups may be used
	3. Expect up-to-date ideas and learning methods	3. May not be approved to cover entire NVQ
	4. Employer may or may not pay	

ALTERNATIVE TYPES OF ASSESSMENT CENTRE contd.

	FOR	AGAINST
Independent training provider	1. May seem closer to workplace than college	1. Training (but not assessment) may feel less monitored than college
	2. Staff may also practice within occupation	
	3. Likely to be smaller organization	2. Atmosphere may not have breadth of college
	4. Has to be good to remain in business	3. May not have equivalent physical resources as larger organization
	5. Smaller organization should be flexible	4. Simulations may be used
	6. Employer may or may not pay	5 May not be approved to cover entire NVQ
	7. Expect up-to-date ideas and learning methods	

NB. All assessment centres have to achieve the same standards set by the awarding body and these are regularly monitored by the awarding body. If you have a choice of assessment centre, you will not so much be choosing between good and bad as between more or less personally suited to you.

5. WHAT DOES THE ASSESSOR DO?

⇨ Guides candidate

⇨ Interprets standards for candidate

⇨ Plans assessment with candidate

⇨ Carries out assessment

⇨ Completes assessment records

⇨ Is qualified in assessment

⇨ Is occupationally competent

⇨ Guides candidate

Your assessor will be your chief guide to the entire NVQ process. For most people the NVQ process itself is a whole new way of life. It is therefore necessary to have an expert guide.

You may be a candidate with little previous experience of training; or you may have experience mainly with traditional qualification systems. Either way, you will need to get your mind around the new NVQ approach.

The ideas behind the approach and the differences between NVQs and traditional qualifications have been explained in the first two chapters of this book. You might want to glance back at some of those listed points just to remind yourself.

Your assessor will remind you that you are being assessed to the national standard – for doing your work to the standard of best current practice. The evidence you collect to prove this will be largely taken from your work, and the qualification when completed will show that you have the necessary skills to carry out your job. The way that you are assessed will be a lot less formal than an examination and you and your assessor will agree the pace at which you should take the NVQ.

⇨ Interprets standards for candidate

When you start to prepare towards your NVQ you will be introduced to a new style of English! Until you have adjusted to the English of occupational standards you will perhaps find it a little strange. When starting the NVQ system it was considered important that all NVQs be written in a standardized way. Rules were established for doing this. The NVQ style can be seen in the example of performance criteria, in Chapter 8.

You will find the way sentences are written rather different from usual. You will also need to become accustomed to interlinking the parts of a standard to make them fit together.

Once you have been shown by your assessor how to do this for the first few standards, the style will become obvious and you will be able to do it for yourself. However, there will be occasions when you are not absolutely certain what the standard requires. At these times your assessor is the interpretation expert whose skills are available to you.

Assessor interprets standards for candidate

● Explains NVQ style of writing
● Shows how sections of standard must be
  interlinked
● Clarifies anything about which the candidate is
  unsure

⇨ Plans assessment with candidate

The assessor will look with you at how many units there are in the NVQ
you want to take. Together you will probably prepare an outline plan
covering all the stages of the NVQ. You will plan in more detail the first
parts on which you have chosen to be assessed.

You will arrange which kinds of evidence will be assessed for the different activities, how much evidence you will need to produce and how
you will arrange it. Naturally you will also arrange mutually convenient times for the assessment – which should always be pre-
arranged and should never be a 'spot check'.

The plan need not be anything sophisticated or complicated. It can
be a straightforward list of which each of you has a copy with dates
jotted down by each stage of the process.

Assessor plans assessment with candidate including:

- Outline plan – can be a simple list
- Early stages in detail
- Types of evidence
- How much evidence
- Arrangement of evidence
- Assessment times – no spot checks

⇨ Carries out assessment

Special assessment guidance notes are an integral part of each NVQ element. Both you, the candidate, and your assessor will use these in the planning process and they will remain a constant source of reference. There are no nasty hidden surprises in NVQs!

There are two kinds of evidence: *performance evidence* and *supplementary evidence*. Performance evidence is the preferred kind as it comes directly from the work itself. It may be that your assessor observes you carrying out some activities or that you present samples of your work as evidence. The amount of performance evidence is laid down in the standard.

Supplementary evidence is rather more indirect which is why it is not the preferred option. It may take the form of informal questioning or verbal or written tests of underpinning knowledge and understanding. You might write a report on something you have done or arrange that a colleague should provide a report as a witness.

You and your assessor have a variety of assessment tools at your disposal. The assessor will look at all the evidence you present and weigh up whether your work matches up yet to the NVQ standard.

Assessor carries out the assessment looking at:

- Performance evidence:
    observation
    work samples
    reports
- Supplementary evidence:
    informal questioning
    verbal tests
    written tests
    witness report

and decides whether your evidence matches the standard

⇨ Completes assessment records

Because NVQs are very significant national qualifications, recording entitlements to them must be carried out very thoroughly. If this were not the case anyone could say they had an NVQ and you might not think it was worth getting one.

Your assessor will be concerned with two main forms for assessing you. The assessor will probably sign one form to indicate your completion of an element and another when you have completed a unit (a set of elements). At the point when the internal verifier (who coordinates and supervises the assessors) checks that the assessor has carried out his/her work properly, the unit form will be countersigned. Within five weeks of completing a unit you should receive a certificate if you wish.

Assessor completes assessment records including:

- Form for element
- Form for unit
- Recommends application for unit certificate

⇨ Is qualified in assessment

The people mainly responsible for running a system based on standards have to be up to standard themselves. Naturally enough, competence-based qualifications have also been developed for assessment and verification. These were drawn up by the Employment Occupational Standards Council (the organization representative of the employment occupational sector with responsibility for NVQ development).

Your assessor will be qualified to 'assess candidate performance' (D32) and to 'assess candidate using differing sources of evidence' (D33). The internal verifier at your assessment centre, will additionally be qualified to 'internally verify the assessment process' (D34). Once you have your NVQ in your chosen occupation, you, too, might wish to qualify as an assessor.

The assessor and internal verifier are qualified in assessment with these NVQ units:

- Assessor:
  D32 Assess candidate performance
  D33 Assess candidate using differing sources of evidence
- Internal verifier:
  D34 Internally verify the assessment process

⇨ **Is occupationally competent**

It seems fairly obvious that if you are being assessed in, for instance, an agricultural occupation, you will not want to be assessed by someone who is qualified in assessment but is an expert in catering! An assessor must therefore be competent in the occupation that she or he is assessing. The awarding body will have a clear definition of occupational competence but it should be borne in mind that it will vary from one area of work to another.

MAITLAND . . . . .

MEMORY JOGGER

Don't forget:

Your assessor is your guide
Your assessor will explain the standards to you
Your assessment is planned jointly between you and your assessor
Your assessor looks at evidence of your competence
Your assessor completes assessment records
Your assessor is expert both in your occupation and in assessment

6. WHAT DOES THE CANDIDATE DO?

⇨ Takes responsibility for the overall process

⇨ Plans assessment with assessor

⇨ Undertakes training to fill gaps

⇨ Gathers evidence

⇨ Organizes evidence

⇨ Takes responsibility for the overall process

As an NVQ candidate you will find that you are responsible for your own training and qualifications. Whether you have been offered the opportunity at work or sought the opportunity elsewhere to take an NVQ, it is yours to take and yours to organize.

You take the process forward after registration by taking advantage

35

of any opportunities offered. Such assistance may take the form of a mentor (an experienced adviser or guide) in addition to your assessor, or assistance with formal or informal training. Your assessment centre should be able to give you at least informal information concerning support services available.

As the person in overall charge of your NVQ, you will need to make sure that all the others concerned in some way with you as a candidate are both consulted and kept informed about what you are doing. When your line manager is not your assessor this is all the more important. The line manager's cooperation in evidence collection, assessment by observation and secondment to necessary training will be essential. The line manager who is kept in the dark cannot be expected to cooperate.

THE CANDIDATE TAKES THE LEAD

- Takes responsibility
- Takes advantage of opportunities offered
- Liaises between all involved

⇨ Plans assessment with assessor

An assessment plan need not be anything very grand or complicated.

Common sense will tell you, however, that if two people are going to work on something together intermittently, they are going to have to agree:

1. when they will do it, and
2. what they will do on each occasion.

So, the assessment plan is likely to include a couple of initial meetings to ensure complete understanding of the standards being assessed, and to agree the likely kinds of evidence that the candidate will need to collect. Some observation sessions may need to be booked and dates agreed by which particular stages will be reached. It could usefully be set out as a plan and assessment diary. The planning information might be held in one column whilst another contains a record of what took place at each point on the plan. Above all you should consider this planning as a negotiation between you and your assessor as partners in the NVQ process.

© PTC

⇨ Undertakes training to fill gaps

You probably don't see much point in taking a qualification that only confirms that what you do, you do well. An NVQ does more than confirm your current skills. New skills augmenting those you already possess are also certificated in an NVQ. The result should be that you may either expand your current job role or apply for other jobs with more scope. This is the pay-off for the extra effort to acquire those new skills.

Earlier in this book, it was explained that training for NVQs need not be through traditional courses. You may find that a colleague is in an ideal position to teach you how to carry out an activity which forms part of your NVQ unit. On the other hand it may be that what you need to learn can be conveniently found in a book or video presentation. If this is the case read or watch it and then try applying what you have learned. Rather more formal ways of filling these gaps may be open or distance learning packages which could include booklets, videos, audio tapes, articles and CD ROMs or computer programs. Some NVQs attract a great many candidates because they apply to a significant part of the working population. These may have learning packages particularly matched to their units. The quality will vary and you may need the expert assistance of a trainer or librarian to select worthwhile material.

DIFFERENT WAYS OF TRAINING

● On the job with colleagues
● From book/video
● By open/distance learning course
● By traditional training course

The luckiest candidates will have training opportunities offered to them through their place of work. If you are one of these, your personnel or training department will have vetted the course offered. If you have to do this for yourself simply treat it as any other product and make some careful enquiries before you sign up – particularly if it is costing a good deal and is going to take up a lot of your time. It's always worth asking to speak to someone who has already been on the course.

You will want to make sure that the content is a close match with the NVQ units you plan to take. You may want to see what other facilities the organization offers to support your learning – a good library or learning resources centre, for example. How many people will attend each class? How much individual help will you be offered? Does the timing suit the rest of your life? In the end you may have to weigh up a course at one place with a good library and a large class, or a course at another with no library but smaller numbers of students. Only you know which will suit you best.

However you choose to acquire those additional skills, remember it is not numbers of books you have read or hours sat in courses that are being assessed. You will be assessed on your application of what you have learned. To this extent any books, videos, trainers or colleagues who have helped you learn are being assessed with you. If you apply what you have learned competently, it suggests that not only you but those who helped you with your training are also competent.

Before signing up for a course ask a former student/trainee:

● Was it value for money?
● Was it worth the time spent?
● Was it a good match with your NVQ units?
● How good were the support facilities?
● How high were the numbers in class?
● Was there much individual help?

Then consider whether the times are convenient for you.

⇨ Gathers evidence

The evidence you collect will fall into two main categories: *performance* and *supplementary evidence*. It may come in any form – written, oral or visual. You are likely to be mainly concerned with the collection of performance evidence, as supplementary evidence will largely be questioning of one sort or another.

Visual evidence does not have to mean your assessor standing there observing you at work. However, this is likely to form some part of the overall assessment. Visual evidence may include photos and videos. Oral evidence could mean your assessor listening to you at work but is equally likely to be a cassette you have recorded yourself. Written evidence may be a report, a memo, a form that has to be completed as a regular part of your job or a report from a colleague or customer about how you have carried out a particular piece of work. Let me provide a few more examples of the kinds of evidence you will collect – these will vary according to the type of work you do.

Perhaps you record statistics, keep records for your organization, keep details of activities within a diary, prepare or contribute to the preparation of budgets or send letters. Many of these will support the units for which you are trying to prepare.

Then again you may deal with work schedules, booking systems, flow charts, plans or layouts. You may have examples of administrative procedures you have helped to set up or operate.

In most jobs, provided that your line manager knows what you are doing, there is unlikely to be a problem in copying sufficient of these kinds of material for your evidence.

People do not always think of their work products as falling under the headings that are mentioned above.

A list of the order in which you deliver meals on wheels, with timings, is a work schedule. A leave book that you keep for the department is an administrative procedure. The movement records of livestock that you complete if you work on a farm will count as statistics collection and record-keeping.

Twenty-five photos of you with your prize herd of cattle or the happy children in your play group will provide no more evidence than one photograph. There is a temptation to feel that the more you show of something, the more believable it is.

Two or three witness reports of your helpful switchboard management should suggest that it is not a rare occurrence for you to be polite and efficient on the telephone, especially if each describes a different situation requiring both tact and persistence. However, ten statements to the effect that you are always efficient and helpful, with no detail, will tell the assessor next to nothing. Evidence must be substantiated so that it may be weighed up as in a court of law.

One telephone message or memo may well provide evidence of several different elements or contribute to the evidence for several different units. Economy with evidence will be applauded, not penalized. It indicates both clear thinking and efficiency. The assessment will be much easier for you and your assessor if you are economical with your evidence. Do not feel obliged to wheel your evidence to your assessor in a supermarket trolley!

© MCI

⇨ Organizes evidence

Just imagine for a moment that your evidence is heaped up in the supermarket trolley. You have done a good job collecting enough of it. What should you do to make it a reasonable collection of material for your assessor to look at?

You will have to divide it into sections and arrange it so that it is easy for the assessor to look up and find particular items. If some pieces of evidence are supporting several activities you will need to provide links, or cross-references, between the evidence and the various elements to which they refer. (For more on organizing evidence, see Chapter 9.)

Further facts for candidates

- Competent candidate implies competent training
- Evidence must be substantiated
- Evidence should be economical
- Evidence should be well organized

SELF-ASSESSMENT

To establish if you are willing to take on the responsibilities of being an NVQ candidate, please complete the following self-assessment checklist.

	Yes	No
Do you want to be in charge of your own career development?	❑	❑
Do you want to plan your own qualifying process in partnership with your assessor?	❑	❑
Are you willing to seek out opportunities to advance your own training?	❑	❑
Would you find it interesting to collect evidence to prove just how competent you are?	❑	❑
Would you find it a challenge to organize that evidence so that it may be assessed easily?	❑	❑

If you answered 'Yes' to most of these questions, then it is time you found out more about what this NVQ actually looks like. So, take a look at the next chapter!

7. WHAT MAKES UP AN NVQ?

⇨ Occupational role

⇨ Units

⇨ Compulsory units

⇨ Optional units

⇨ Elements

⇨ Occupational role

Each NVQ reflects a group of jobs of a particular level within one occupational area. Looking at the different levels of NVQ covering your kind of work, it should be possible to recognize where your own job fits. However, no qualification will be so specific as to reflect a single job held by one person only (this would be neither economic nor practical). There should be sufficient room within each NVQ for it to apply to a great many people's jobs.

⇨ Units

A unit is the smallest part of an NVQ for which you can be awarded a certificate. Occasionally it will reflect the whole of a very specialized job or, more usually, a particular aspect of a more broadly based job.

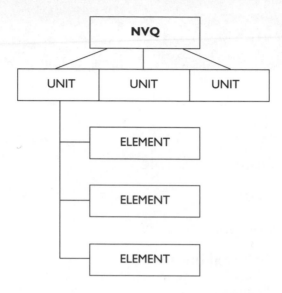

'Process documents relating to goods and services' (Administration, level 2, unit 10) includes two elements. The first is 'order goods and services', the second is 'process claims for payment'. Many post-holders in administration departments spend most of their working lives ordering equipment for the rest of the organization and would choose to be certificated for taking this one unit. On the other hand, many secretaries include this activity within a much wider role for a small office or in an organization where such functions are not carried out by specialists. Such a secretary would take the level 2 NVQ, choosing the unit mentioned as her optional unit, and taking the eight compulsory units (see below).

Typically an NVQ will include 6 to 12 units. However, they vary according to occupation and level. To be certain, you will have to check up on the NVQ that particularly interests you.

Most of the units in your NVQ have been especially developed for your kind of work. However, some units will have been adopted from NVQs drawn up for other occupational areas, or from the generic qualifications such as Customer Service, Management, IT, and Administration, which are activities that pervade almost all kinds of work. Other units, such as those in foreign languages, may be taken additionally to more closely reflect a specialization. A person whose occupation involves, for example, regular use of the Russian language would take his or her NVQ in the specialist occupation and an additional unit of Russian in which some of the appropriate technical vocabulary would be included. In this way it should be possible to finely tune an NVQ so that it works for you.

⇨ Compulsory units

Some NVQs are made up entirely of units which you have to take; there is no choice. These are called *mandatory* units. However, you should find that these compulsory units reflect the core of your occupation. At least half the units of an NVQ will be compulsory. Every candidate for an NVQ will take this group of units.

⇨ Optional units

Acknowledging that the emphasis of different jobs, even at the same level, will vary, many NVQs will also have a range of alternative units from which you may select a certain number. Sometimes in the interest of a broad-based qualification you will be directed to take one optional unit from each group of units on a list, in much the same way as schools do when asking pupils to choose from groups of possible GCSEs. Sometimes it is possible to slant the NVQ very much towards a particular area of specialism. Level 4, Periodical (magazine) advertisement production, offers an optional unit: 'Ensuring the maintenance of production quality: colour correction'. This is clearly an important specialist activity within the magazine industry.

⇨ Elements

Each unit consists of a number of elements. These are the smallest meaningful activities identified during the process of NVQ development. (There is more on elements in the next chapter.)

If you think of a domestic activity such as preparing a drink – which is familiar and straightforward, you will begin to realize that it includes a range of skills according to the type of drink being prepared. So the activity of preparing a drink is a *function*. On the other hand, in the preparation of a specific drink, for example, instant coffee, a whole series of *tasks* must be carried out. These will include running the tap, putting water in the kettle, switching the kettle on, taking the lid off the jar of coffee and placing a spoonful of coffee in the mug. People often confuse functions and tasks.

NVQs are about functions which are fairly complex groups of activities describing their purpose and result. The function of preparing a drink is a complete activity seen through from beginning to end with a clear purpose and result. Too much attention to the detailed tasks of running the tap or boiling the water could lead to these being seen as ends in themselves, forgetful of the real purpose of preparing a drink. We all know people who seem to run round in circles so absorbed in the detail of what they are doing that they know longer seem to know why they are doing it!

MEMORY JOGGER

Don't forget:

Each NVQ reflects a group of job roles
Each NVQ has a number of units
Some units are compulsory
Some units are optional
Each unit has a number of elements
NVQs are concerned with functions – far more complex than tasks

8. WHAT MAKES UP AN ELEMENT?

- ➯ Element title
- ➯ Performance Criteria
- ➯ Range
- ➯ Underpinning knowledge and understanding
- ➯ Assessment requirements

Throughout this chapter the examples used come from Administration level 1, Unit 4: Develop effective working relationships. (National standards for administration: level 1. Administration Lead Body, 1995.)

➯ Element title

The element title simply summarizes the activity being carried out by the candidate who is being assessed for the element.

Element 4.2: Greet and assist visitors

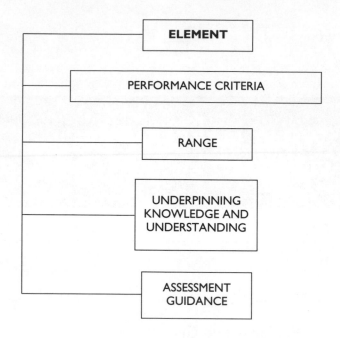

⇨ Performance Criteria

Performance Criteria are a list of the *outcomes* or *results* of activities undertaken to complete an element. The Performance Criteria below would be carried out by a receptionist in some organizations and in others by a porter or a secretary.

(a) *Visitors are greeted promptly and courteously and their needs identified.*
(b) *Visitors are given only disclosable information.*
(c) *Visitors are directed or escorted to destination, as required.*
(d) *Reasons for delay or unavailability of assistance are explained politely.*
(e) *Situations outside own responsibility are referred to the appropriate person.*
(f) *Methods of communication and support are suited to the needs of the visitors*

These criteria alone would suggest that you work like a machine. As NVQs describe complex work carried out by people, not the relatively simple work of machines, they link several different aspects of people's work activities.

⇨ Range

The Range statements (called 'Range indicators' in certain NVQs), flesh out Performance Criteria. This is done by putting them into the context of different work situations.

Visitors:
Expected visitors
Unexpected visitors

Each time you come across the word 'visitors' in the Performance Criteria, replace it with each of the alternatives from the Range. You will nearly double the number of Performance Criteria (the section above) by taking into account *expected* and *unexpected* visitors. (Read in conjunction with Evidence requirements (ii), p.50.)

⇨ Underpinning knowledge and understanding (UKU)

NVQs are not only about doing. You will realize that however practical you are about carrying out your work well, you cannot do it well without understanding what you are doing and why you are doing it. You must also be conversant with any regulations concerning your own work activities.

The words 'theory', 'learning' and 'principles' probably equate with Underpinning Knowledge and Understanding. The difference is largely in the means by which your competence in this area will be confirmed. The traditional way has been to test a large body of knowledge for its own sake. The NVQ way is to incorporate evidence of UKU into the assessment of performance.

It may be more convenient to acquire the formal underpinning knowledge separately for your unit, or even your entire NVQ.

- Recognition and reaction to verbal and nonverbal communication
- Communications with persons having special communication needs
- Assistance with mobility of persons having special mobility needs
- Effective spoken communication
- Rules on confidentiality of information
- Security procedures
- Structure, location and responsibilities of relevant people in the organization
- Greeting style/s used by organization
- Employee responsibilities in complying with equal opportunities legislation
- Own responsibilities in complying with organization's policies and procedures with regard to visitors

(Read this UKU in conjunction with Evidence requirement (iv), below.)

⇨ Assessment requirements

An important feature of the NVQ system is its lack of surprise. The method of the assessment is laid down within each element. At the end of each element is a specification of how much evidence of each type is required.

Evidence requirements

(i)   All performance criteria must be met.
(ii)   Evidence must be available to prove that all variables within the range have been included in the assessment.
(iii) Competence must be demonstrated consistently, over a period of time, with evidence of performance obtained from a variety of sources.
(iv)   Evidence for the listed knowledge and understanding must be made available where it is not apparent from performance.
(v)   Performance evidence must be available of the candidate greeting visitors courteously and assisting them, within limits of own authority.

Assessment guidance

The following are potential sources of evidence, but candidates and assessors may be able to identify other, appropriate sources:

- *Observed performance, eg*
  - *greeting visitors on arrival at workplace – visitors from within and/or from outside the organization*
  - *putting visitors at ease*
  - *finding out reasons for visit – business, appointment, information*
  - *dealing with unexpected visitors*
  - *directing or escorting visitors to other staff and/or locations*
  - *responding, within limits of own authority, to questions about the organization, its products and services*
  - *assisting visitors with additional needs – physical, sensory, language*
  - *referring visitors to other staff when their requirements are beyond own capability or authority*
- *Work products, eg*
  - *office records of visitors*
- *Authenticated testimonies from relevant witnesses, eg*
  - *supervisor*
- *Personal accounts of competence*
- *Responses to questions*
- *Other sources of evidence to prove knowledge and understanding where it is not apparent from performance*

While NVQs are best assessed in the workplace they can also include tests. These may be fairly formal or they could simply be an informal question and answer session – a fairly searching talk with your assessor.

Remember that the full range does not have to be assessed as a result of performance: a stated proportion may be judged on supplementary or knowledge evidence.

PROGRESS LIST

This progress list is here to remind you what you will learn about NVQs in this book and what stage you have reached so far.

☑ What is an NVQ?

☑ Why take an NVQ?

☑ How to become an NVQ candidate

☑ What is an assessment centre?

☑ Where is an assessment centre?

☑ What does the assessor do?

☑ What does the candidate do?

☑ What makes up an NVQ?

☑ What makes up an element?

☐ A portfolio?

☐ What next?

☐ The NVQ framework

☐ Persuading your boss about NVQs

Where to find out more
Abbreviations and jargon

Now you know what an NVQ is. Next you are going to find out the reasons for registering as a candidate.

9. A PORTFOLIO?

➡ Work project not school project

➡ Contents

➡ Career history

➡ Context of assessment

➡ Assessment forms

➡ Evidence

➡ Arrangement of portfolio

➡ Useful after assessment

All you need to start work on your portfolio is: a ring binder, dividers, a hole punch, a glue stick, clear plastic pockets, plain white and coloured paper, coloured labels and coloured pens.

⇨ Work project not school project

If you have children of school age or if you are of the generation that has done a good deal of project work during your own school education, you will quickly take to the portfolio. It is literally the work version of a school project! Just like a school project a portfolio is a convenient way of arranging a great variety of material. The successful portfolio shows that you have really got under the skin of the area about which you have been learning.

If you are not familiar with school projects, the portfolio concept may be a little harder to grasp. Art students will take a selection of their work in a portfolio to an interview, whether for a place at college or for a job, to prove their standard and range of ability. This is largely because a few sentences on a piece of paper or a single examination grade are quite insufficient as a means of demonstrating practical ability. Your portfolio as an NVQ candidate will also be used as proof of how well you carry out your work.

However, the NVQ portfolio is not a random selection so much as a concise collection of evidence of your ability to carry out the requirements of a specific unit, or group of units, towards an NVQ. Most often, like the school project, it will be held in a ring binder. However, some bulky items, such as videos, may not fit into it but this does not matter. You will simply find another container.

PORTFOLIO

- Consists of a variety of material
- Comprises a concise collection
- Is like an artist's portfolio
- Is proof of ability and understanding
- Is usually contained in a ring binder

⇨ **Contents**

First you will need a title page, as in any book, which will give your own details and those of the NVQ unit to which the portfolio refers. Next comes a contents list. This should itemize the main headings but not every scrap of information within the binder. The list will follow the order of arrangement within the binder and lead the assessor to the page number or the section where the particular area of information starts.

Like everything else within your portfolio, the contents list is included to make it easier for your assessor to find his or her way through your evidence. The contents list is a major signpost.

PORTFOLIO CONTENTS LIST

- Is a signpost
- Includes main headings
- Is in order of arrangement
- Is easy for reader to follow

⇨ **Career history**

It is not essential to include in your portfolio an outline of your career. However, particularly if your assessor does not already know you very well, this could provide a much more rounded picture of you and your working life. It may save you answering some queries yourself. More importantly, if you are largely being assessed on the basis of your port-folio but are not necessarily sitting there while it is being studied, it will give the assessor the chance to get to know you in your absence.

You may already have a curriculum vitae (CV) prepared. Check it, and update it if necessary. If you do not already have one, prepare a simple list of the jobs you have done, and include your job title, the name of the organization for which you were working, and the dates you worked there. When the job seems particularly relevant to the NVQ you are taking, be sure to include details of your main duties and experience of value in the NVQ. Details of relevant qualifications you have already taken should be included as these may help you to prove your Underpinning Knowledge and Understanding. A CV can be lengthy and complicated. However, for this purpose it should be brief and straightforward. You might like to attach a photo of yourself – again, it can help your assessor.

CAREER HISTORY

- Rounded picture of you
- Up-to-date
- Relevant jobs and achievements listed
- Relevant main duties outlined
- Relevant qualifications listed
- Brief and straightforward

⇨ Context of assessment

This section is an opportunity for you to write one or two paragraphs describing the background to your current job situation in which you are being assessed for your NVQ. Describe, insofar as it is relevant, the organization in which you are being assessed. You may wish to include an organization chart showing your own position as well as outlining the type and size of organization. Your job description would be useful here. If there are regular witness statements from the same people included in your portfolio, it would be helpful to give some information to put them in context.

If your assessor is your line manager it may seem odd to explain what you do and where and why you do it – after all, your line manager should know! However, the internal verifier, who may be further away from you within the organization, may not know much about what you do. The internal verifier oversees the assessor. For the candidate who is registered at an assessment centre outside the place of work it will be vital to explain the context in which the evidence has been collected. The external verifier, who comes to the assessment centre on behalf of the awarding body, will also need this background information. The external verifier oversees and advises the assessment centre.

Consider what you write on context to be your opportunity to point out anything that may need explaining. Perhaps some jobs are done seasonally and others occur very rarely. Possibly you have a special skill or unusual experience.

CONTEXT INCLUDES:

- The organization in which you gathered your evidence
- Where you fit in the organization
- Background to witnesses who have provided assessment evidence for your portfolio
- What you do and why you do it

and the context should make the portfolio easier for the reader to understand

⇨ Assessment forms

Awarding bodies and individual assessment centres may vary in the number and arrangement of their assessment forms. At the least you must expect to complete a form for each element and often another one summarizing each unit. Your assessor will make sure that you understand how to do this. For your own purposes you may prepare additional forms yourself to standardize the format in which you provide certain types of evidence, for example, witness reports.

Just like the contents list, these forms should be viewed as signposts.

The unit form is likely to appear the least complicated and will provide an overview. The form completed for each element will ensure that every performance criteria has been checked against each item of Range and Underpinning Knowledge and Understanding. It is also a cross-referencing list, referring the reader of your portfolio to the individual items of evidence supporting the element being assessed. You will need to give each item of evidence a unique reference number so that it may be cross-referenced to more than one element.

At first glance the element form may appear slightly daunting. If you think of it as the main link between the various parts of the element and your collection of evidence, then it should begin to make sense. There are so many strands involved that it has to have a good many columns. This is the point at which the assessor is able to cross-check that everything has been covered. The element forms are the links holding the portfolio together.

ASSESSMENT FORMS

- Provide signposts through the evidence
- May be expected at least for units and elements
- Act as the main links in a portfolio
- Contain a unique reference number for each item of evidence

---

⇨ Evidence

You should select your evidence economically for its value as proof of your competence in a particular aspect of an element. It is only useful if it is specific. In Chapter 6 it was explained that evidence for your assessment may be written, oral or visual. You will have no trouble placing sheets of written information or photographs in your ring binder portfolio. More difficult may be the video, cassette or large plan. There is no problem with any of these formats provided they contain valuable evidence.

You will need to be a little more imaginative in finding a means of storage and arrangement for bulkier kinds of evidence. If they are held in a separate container, this must be indicated on the element form. Each item of evidence will be identified on the element form by its unique reference number.

Evidence should be dated and, if it is from a team exercise (perhaps a report of a meeting in which you took part), the extent of your contribution needs to be confirmed. Your evidence should show that you are currently competent. This means that if you are including Accreditation of Prior Learning (APL) in your portfolio, this prior skill must be shown to still be relevant. APL means the formal acknowledgement of evidence of skills you already possess. These skills must be to the level of the current national standard.

EVIDENCE SHOULD BE:

Economical
Well stored
Uniquely referenced by number
Current
Still relevant if APL
Confirmed if teamwork

⇨ Arrangement of portfolio

Your goal in choosing how to arrange your portfolio is to make it easy for your assessor to find things. Several alternative arrangements will probably occur to you as you are gathering your work together.

Provided that goal is foremost in your mind, it does not matter which means you choose. At the outset, however, you should explain your method of arrangement and also provide a key to abbreviations and jargon. If you are certain these terms are used throughout your occupation your assessor and verifiers should be fully conversant with them. However, some jargon and abbreviations will be used within your organization only and the external verifier cannot be expected to understand these – no more can your assessor if you are using an assessment centre outside your workplace.

You might decide to file all the evidence relating to one element behind its form. If so do not forget when a piece of evidence relates to more than one element (a letter, memo or report will often refer to more than one activity) that although it can only be filed in one place, your cross-referencing should make it easy to find from other points in the portfolio.

Alternatively you may decide that the easiest method of arrangement is by type of evidence. You place all records of telephone calls together, all photographs together, all memos, budgets, reports of meetings, and so on in separate sections. Once again with clear cross-referencing it should be straightforward to link back from the element form.

Colour will not only brighten up your portfolio but will also provide an additional means of leading your assessor through it. A particular colour might indicate the format of the evidence or it might be chosen to represent a particular element so that everything relating to it is marked with that colour. Like all other signposting, colour coding can be invaluable provided that it is logical, clear and consistent.

Have a look in a good stationers and buy a range of materials to help you to make your portfolio easy to follow and so attractive to look at that you feel it is an achievement in itself, of which you may be justifiably proud.

One word of warning – do not make your portfolio over-complicated!

Arrangement of portfolio should be:

- Made easy for assessor
- Explained: arrangement, referencing, abbreviations, jargon
- Arranged logically
- Colour coded
- Not over-complicated

⇨ **Useful after assessment**

Some organizations will be introducing NVQs as part of a new approach to personnel and training based entirely upon the occupational standards. In these organizations you will expect to take your current portfolio to performance reviews and appraisals. They will provide a focus for the discussion.

If, however, you work for an organization that is not itself an assessment centre, your line manager may not be familiar with NVQ portfolios. It might be something to take along and offer to look at in the appraisal. If your work does not normally include the arrangement of documents, writing or photography – all of which skills have been necessary to build up the portfolio – this will be a way of drawing to your boss's attention these previously hidden abilities. Your work too is likely to gain renewed respect when well presented on paper. It is very easy for others to forget just how many components there are to your job.

Similarly, your portfolio is something to take with you to an interview for a prospective new job. Again, it will provide a focus, and while you will not expect the interviewer to read it page by page, your portfolio should give an impression of a well-organized person able to present yourself and your ideas well. You should know your own way round it very well so that you can quickly turn up an item in support of a point you are making in conversation.

A good portfolio will take time and trouble to prepare. Make it work for you!

After assessment the portfolio:

● May be used at appraisal
● Shows additional organizational skills
● Provides status for work
● May be used at interviews

SHOPPING LIST
FOR
PORTFOLIO STARTER KIT

Ring binder
Dividers
Hole punch
Glue stick
Clear plastic pockets
Plain white paper
Plain coloured paper
Coloured pens
Coloured labels

This list will start you off but as time goes on you will devise your own way of designing your portfolio.

10. WHAT NEXT?

➡️ Certificate for unit

➡️ Build units into NVQ

or

➡️ Select units from different sectors

➡️ Certificate for unit

You do not have to set aside years of your life to work for an NVQ. Every time you are assessed as competent in all the elements that make up a unit, you will be certificated. You should consider this unit as a mini qualification in its own right, awarded for the particular skill in which you have been assessed. On its own a unit certificate is something to prove your ability if, for instance, you are applying for a promotion or a new job.

⇨ **Build units into NVQ**

Most candidates will probably be aiming for a whole NVQ. Depending on the level of NVQ – and therefore the complexity and difficulty of the work – the number of units, or elements within each unit, may increase.

At the end of building up the necessary number of units you will be assessed in your work as competent to a particular level. This assessment is likely to provide you and your job with a status. You should find it easier to gauge your own level and that of your job in relation to others, particularly in relation to promotions or job moves.

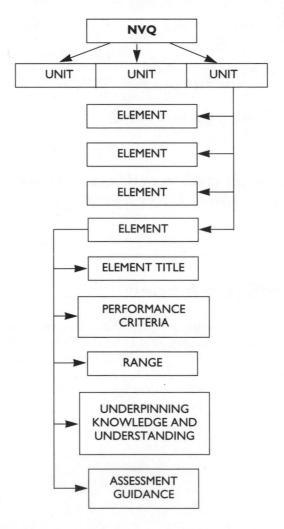

➪ **Select units from different sectors**

Some jobs just do not fit tidily into an exact NVQ. While the aim in devising the system has been to reflect the real job situation, a national system could not hope to encompass every single job in existence.

Think of a post advertised as Secretary/Information Assistant, for example. It is very likely that such a job would in part be reflected by an Administration NVQ (these cover standard secretarial posts) and additionally, because there is a clear emphasis on information, some units from an Information and Library Services NVQ. It sounds as if the holder of a job like this will find the information handling unit from Administration insufficiently detailed. On the other hand, taking a complete Information and Library Services NVQ would exaggerate the information component of the job.

Other jobs people hold will have an even greater mix of activities within them. If yours is one of these I expect it will be reflected in a selection of units from an assortment of occupations. On the other hand you may prefer to try to get the necessary experience to gain a whole NVQ in the area of work most emphasized within your job. The choice has to be yours.

However, a mixed bag of units from different work areas will demonstrate your skills but will not make it easy for a future employer to gauge the level at which you operate. Units do not have levels. Only whole NVQs are assigned to levels (see p.68 for more about levels).

There is also the likelihood that the selection of units that so well reflects your current job may be so specialized as to reflect no other job in existence! If you think this may be the case, seek advice from the assessment centre at which you were thinking of registering. The staff there will be able to advise you how to maximize the benefits of NVQ units from the point of view of your own career.

YOUR CHECKLIST OF ALTERNATIVES

You will have to decide whether it is more practical for you to:
– get one certificate for a particular skill that you prize
– collect a variety of unit certificates from the different areas of work you cover
– work towards a whole NVQ.

11. THE NVQ FRAMEWORK

⇨ More like a climbing frame

⇨ Upward progression

⇨ Sideways progression

⇨ Comparable and transferable skills

⇨ More like a climbing frame

With what should the flexible NVQ system be compared? It is not like a snakes and ladders board because, unlike the traditional qualifications systems in which examination failure is not uncommon, there are no snakes to fall down!

Nor is it a ladder. Some candidates may well choose to progress upwards and achieve higher and higher levels of certification in their chosen field. Others may prefer breadth to height, and progress sideways, broadening their skills base.

Many candidates, like children on a climbing frame, will sometimes move up and sometimes across. This will be true when a candidate is seeking to show an ability to transfer between job types.

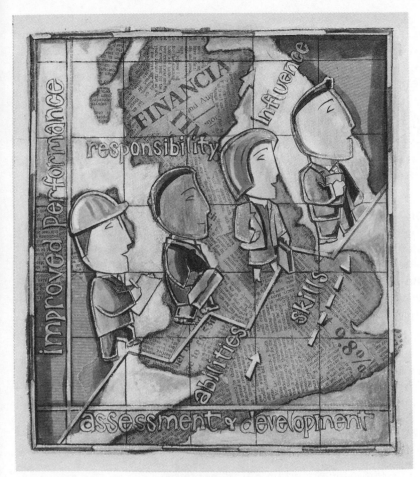

© MCI

⇨ Upward progression

There are five levels of NVQ. Not all have been developed in every occupation and indeed some levels will never be prepared for some occupations.

The NVQ ladder may be joined at any rung which seems the appropriate point for you. It is not always necessary to work through from level 1 to level 5.

The definitions below describing NVQ levels are the official ones laid down by the National Council for Vocational Qualifications. They come from NVQ Criteria and Guidance, published by NCVQ in 1995. Like much 'Civil Service speak' they are not an example of clarity. Your assessor should be able to tell you how they apply to you. I have added some headings in italic as a quick guide to what the different levels mean.

Routine work
Level 1: competence which involves the application of knowledge in the performance of a range of varied work activities, most of which may be routine or predictable.

Some varied work with responsibility
Level 2: competence which involves the application of knowledge in a significant range of varied work activities, performed in a variety of contexts. Some of the activities are complex or non-routine, and there is some individual responsibility or autonomy. Collaboration with others, perhaps through membership of a work group or team, may often be a requirement.

Some supervision of others
Level 3: competence which involves the application of knowledge in a broad range of varied work activities performed in a wide variety of contexts, most of which are complex and non-routine. There is considerable responsibility and autonomy, and control or guidance of others is often required.

Junior professional work/junior management
Level 4: competence which involves the application of knowledge in a broad range of complex, technical or professional work activities performed in a wide variety of contexts and with a substantial degree of personal responsibility and autonomy. Responsibility for the work of others and the allocation of resources is often present.

Experienced professional work/management
Level 5: competence which involves the application of a significant range of fundamental principles across a wide and often unpredictable variety of contexts. Very substantial personal autonomy and often significant responsibility for the work of others and for the allocation of substantial resources feature strongly, as do personal accountabilities for analysis and diagnosis, design, planning, execution and evaluation.

REASONS FOR SIDEWAYS PROGRESSION

- career change
- occupation demands new skills:
  computing
  commercial skill

⇨ Sideways progression

Nowadays many of us will change the course of our careers several times. Some skills become redundant and the market grows for others.

As organizations and jobs within them develop, so staff have to acquire new and often very different skills. A good example of this is how since the mid-1970s increasing numbers of people have had to acquire computer skills.

Similarly, since about 1980 many people working in previously 'free to the customer' services have had their roles widened to encompass a commercial side. Examples of this can be found in education, librarianship and museum work.

⇨ The skills are comparable, and sometimes transferable

The whole NVQ framework (below) shows that there are 11 broad areas of competence. Within each of these areas are five levels of achievement. There are about 160 sets of qualifications available now, or ready soon (a list is provided on p.87). As it is possible to move between areas of competence, up and down levels of achievement, and between 160 sets of qualifications, the possible scope is enormous.

The 11 areas of competence in the NVQ framework are:

Tending animals, plants and land	Providing goods and services
Extracting and providing natural resources	Providing health, social care and protective services
Constructing	Providing business services
Engineering	Communicating
Manufacturing	Developing and extending
Transporting	knowledge and skill

A huge effort has been made to keep the rules of assessment standard between all areas of competence. The aim has been to arrive at a system in which the amount of skill required for a level 2 in Racehorse care is exactly comparable with the skill required for a level 2 qualification in customer care (through a Customer Service NVQ).

Not all the efforts have been successful, but the effort has been made. This means that holders of level 2 qualifications in closely similar areas of competence – for instance hotel reception and retail – might be expected to transfer their jobs without much difficulty.

Also, some skills – like data handling, which comes into Administration at level 2 – are obviously transferable across a large number of areas of competence. Once you have been assessed as competent in one of these units, you do not need to be reassessed in it, even if it appears in another NVQ which you decide to take.

SUMMARY OF THE NVQ FRAMEWORK

- Five levels
- 11 areas of competence
- 160+ groups of qualifications under development
- All levels of skill are comparable
- Some skills are transferable

SELF-ASSESSMENT

Start to work out where you fit in the framework!

You can choose between 5 levels of difficulty:

☐ Level 1

☐ Level 2

☐ Level 3

☐ Level 4

☐ Level 5

and between 11 areas of competence:

☐ Tending animals, plants and land

☐ Extracting and providing natural resources

☐ Constructing

☐ Engineering

☐ Manufacturing

☐ Transporting

☐ Providing goods and services

☐ Providing health, social care and protective services

☐ Providing business services

☐ Communicating

☐ Developing and extending knowledge and skill

and within the areas of competence about 160 groups of qualifications. These are listed on pp.87–88. Start to find out about the ones that interest you.

12. PERSUADING YOUR BOSS ABOUT NVQs

⇨ Higher quality output

⇨ Better motivated staff

⇨ Staff training programme towards national qualifications

⇨ Senior staff freed for new work as they can delegate more

⇨ NVQs provide structure for many personnel and training functions

⇨ Plan strategy

⇨ Obtain guidance

⇨ Plan how to fill training gaps

⇨ Higher quality output

Wherever you work it's a certainty that your boss will be looking for more and better outputs from the organization as a whole. The changes taking place at the moment, both in terms of customer expectations and the technology to meet the requirements are phenomenal. Changes in your work style for both these reasons will be continuous, and to manage these your learning will need to be continuous and to high current standards.

NVQs have been developed to meet these needs. The time for burying heads in the sand is over – unless they are going to remain in the sand for ever!

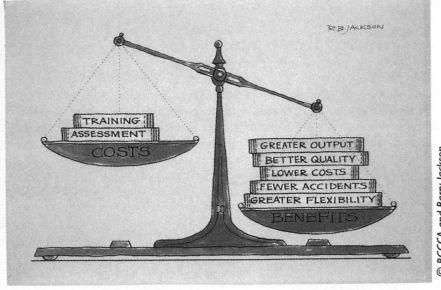

© BCCCA and Barry Jackson

NVQs WILL ASSIST HIGHER QUALITY OUTPUT

- More and better outputs expected
- Changes in customer expectations
- Changes in technology
- Changes in work style needed
- Continuous learning to high standards needed

⇨ Better motivated staff

The stimulus of following a well planned programme of training is bound to revive your interest in your work. Assistance to keep up with what is new and the opportunity to extend your abilities and skills are likely to make you more enthusiastic about the organization making this training available to you. This in turn makes you a more valuable employee.

NVQs RESULT IN BETTER MOTIVATED STAFF

- Well planned training programme
- Staff's abilities maintained and extended
- Staff more enthusiastic
- Employees become more valuable

⇨ Staff training programme towards national qualifications

Training is all very well, but training leading to a national qualification is something staff can keep as their own. Job applicants will be able to prove the training they have undergone which will be helpful for both the employer and employee. This will make it easier for employees to move around and therefore easier, too, for employers to find new staff. Obtaining a national qualification as a result of training will add credibility to the training itself, and make it more highly valued by staff.

TRAINING TOWARDS A NATIONAL QUALIFICATION

- Job applicants will have proof of skills
- Staff become more mobile
- New staff easier to find
- Staff value training more

⇨ Senior staff freed for new work as they can delegate more

As staff at lower levels are trained to carry out more complex work, and technology takes over a great deal that is routine, so the more senior staff in your organization will be able to delegate more of their own work. This in turn will release those senior staff to carry out new functions, look harder for new markets, and so on. The overall effect of NVQs is to increase the skills of the entire workforce and enable more to share responsibility.

SENIOR STAFF CAN DELEGATE MORE

- Technology carries out much of routine
- Lower levels trained to carry out more complex work
- Senior staff freed for new functions and to seek new markets
- Entire workforce increases skills

⇨ **NVQs provide structure for many personnel and training functions**

Personnel and training departments of organizations looking at NVQs for the first time should consider them as a new structure on which to hang many of their human resource management functions. The standards developed in the process of creating NVQs are an excellent management tool in their own right. They provide an immediate basis for carrying out a training needs analysis and from this may be devised your organization's whole training policy.

A great deal of time is spent writing what are often not very clear job descriptions. Once again, much of this work may be reduced by using the occupational standards as the basis.

Recruitment procedures will be a good deal more streamlined when the skills required may be explained in terms of NVQs, and skills offered by applicants explained as NVQ attainment will be immediately clear to employers.

Once in a job there is the regular appraisal routine – all too often a situation which no one knows how to handle properly. NVQs will provide a focal point for these reviews. How do an employee's skills measure up to those specified as necessary for the job? Is the assessment plan on target? For those who find the appraisal process difficult there is a new point upon which it may focus – the portfolio. Instead of awkward attempts at relaxed conversation, how about looking through the NVQ portfolio, so bringing the reality of the job into the appraisal interview?

MAITLAND....

© BLC

NVQ standard as a management tool for:

● Training needs analysis
● Improved job descriptions
● Streamlined recruitment procedures
● Point of focus for appraisals

⇨ **Plan strategy**

If you are trying to persuade your boss that your organization should become an assessment centre for NVQs you will need to understand the process yourself. It will take the most determined organization some time if it is starting from scratch – so don't expect to start on your NVQ next week if your organization is not yet an assessment centre!

If you work for a large organization it may already be approved as an assessment centre for some NVQs but not for others. If it is not approved for the one you and your colleagues want to take but the same awarding body offers it, the process will be a lot quicker.

If there are only a few people in your organization who are likely to take the NVQ you want, your boss might do better to assist you to use a centre elsewhere, such as a college or an independent training organization.

Many organizations contain small specialist departments servicing their main business. Major retail groups have selling as their main activity. Approval for assessment for selling makes sense. It is likely that such a group would also wish to assess buying, administration and management. However, it might not have enough potential candidates to make accounting, design or information and library services viable for in-house assessment. For such candidates it might be more sensible to purchase the services of other providers. Another option would be to join a consortium assessment centre. (See Chapter 4 on the different types of centre available.)

No matter which course your boss decides to follow, it will still be necessary to plan a careful strategy.

- What does the organization expect to gain from NVQs?
- How many staff are likely to take an NVQ?
- Will an experimental trial be run before the whole organization starts to use NVQs?
- Will the trial use staff from one department or a member of staff from every department?
- Over how long a period will the pilot run?
- Will it rely on volunteers?
- How will its value to the organization be assessed?
- Who will take the lead?
- What support will be given to candidates?
- What are the resourcing implications?

A glance at this list, which is by no means exhaustive, will make you realize that a good deal is involved.

PLAN STRATEGY

Allow time
● Find out whether already centre for some NVQs
Consider numbers of candidates
Consider use of another centre
Consider membership of consortium
Find means of gauging organizational gains
Consider NVQ trial first
Provide support to candidates
Obtain resourcing

⇨ Obtain guidance

Your employer, like you, will have a number of different organizations to turn to for advice. The National Council for Vocational Qualifications (NCVQ) or the local Training and Enterprise Council (TEC) will be able to supply general information such as which NVQs are available, which Lead Body developed them and which awarding bodies offer them. The TEC is likely to be able to provide information on other organizations in the same area offering the NVQ your organization is contemplating. Detailed information will be available from the appropriate Lead Body and awarding body. NVQs which cover the work of a large part of the working population are frequently offered by several awarding bodies.

Your employer will be able to receive details of coverage of the NVQ, the direct costs and application forms from the awarding body. It is the expert organization in all aspects concerning administration and assessment of the NVQ. The Lead Body, which represents the work area, may be able to give practical guidance based on the experience of how others have done it. Both should be actively trying to encourage take-up.

The awarding body, for a modest fee, will often be able to offer a single advisory visit to a prospective centre. Some organizations, however, without the spare staff to put into planning for NVQs and with no previous experience, may prefer to obtain consultancy help through the planning and introductory period.

Your organization can obtain guidance from:

● NCVQ
● the local TEC
● the appropriate Lead Body
● the awarding body for the particular NVQ

⇨ Plan how to fill training gaps

You will no doubt be persuading your boss that NVQs are less disruptive to work flow – and more relevant to the workplace – than traditional day-release courses. However, there is no point in trying to hide the fact that to achieve NVQs training will undoubtedly be necessary.

Whether the training is carried out by your line manager at the same time as doing the job, whether computer-assisted learning facilities or video training are supplied at work, whether trainers are brought in or you are sent out for training, it will still cost both time and money. The idea behind the NVQ movement is to improve the skills of the working population and so make it produce to higher levels of quality and efficiency. You donít do this by only giving out certificates. To be entitled to the certificates, staff must work to national standards and it is in the interests of their employers to help staff to achieve these.

⇨ **Final word**

You may by now be thinking, 'This sounds great from my boss's point of view but how about me?' Well, the whole point is that NVQs will be good for you both.

You now know how to get an NVQ and how to introduce your organization to the idea of becoming part of the NVQ world. Early on in this book you read that NVQs are about doing. So have a look at the last three reference sections and then go out and do. *Go and get yourself registered for an NVQ!*

WHERE TO FIND OUT MORE

Regulatory bodies

National Council of Vocational Qualifications (NCVQ)
222 Euston Road, London, NW1 2BZ
Tel. 0171 387 9898; Fax. 0171 387 0978

Scotvec
Hanover House
24 Douglas Street, Glasgow, G2 7NQ
Tel. 0141 242 2171; Fax. 0141 242 2244

Overseas enquiries
NVQ Development Unit
The British Council
10 Spring Gardens, London, SW1A 2BN
Tel. 0171 389 4178; Fax. 0171 389 4589

Awarding bodies

There are a great many awarding bodies. Those listed here, between them cover a large proportion of available NVQs. If none of them offers the one you are interested in, you can get the necessary details from NCVQ, the relevant Lead Body or ITO.

Business and Technology Education Council (BTEC)
Central House, Upper Woburn Place
London, WC1H OHH
Tel. 0171 413 8400; Fax. 0171 413 8430

City and Guilds of London Institute (CGLI)
76 Portland Place, London, W1N 4AA
Tel. 0171 278 2468; Fax. 0171 436 7630

RSA Examination Board
Westwood Way, Coventry, C4 8HS
Tel. 01203 470033; Fax. 01203 468080

Scotvec
Hanover House
24 Douglas Street, Glasgow, G2 7NQ
Tel. 0141 242 2171; Fax. 0141 242 2244

Training and Enterprise Councils

It should be possible to obtain the address of the TEC (LEC in Scotland) from your telephone directory, library or town hall. You may receive assistance from the TEC covering the area in which you live or in which you work.

TEC National Council
Westminster Tower
3 Albert Embankment, London, SE1 7SX
Tel. 0171 735 0010; Fax. 0171 735 0090

Industry Training Organizations and Lead Bodies

In the first instance you may obtain the address of the ITO or Lead Body for your sector from your local TEC, NCVQ or Scotvec. An alternative source of information is NCITO.

National Council of Industry Training Organizations (NCITO)
10 Amos Road
Unit 10 Meadowcourt, Sheffield, S9 1BX
Tel. 01742 619926; Fax. 01742 618103

Selected publications

There is a considerable range of books on NVQs aimed at trainers and employers but very little on the open market available for candidates. Awarding bodies and Lead Bodies involved in your chosen NVQ will be able to supply leaflets, newsletters and scheme books which, in addition to the units, will provide some guidance. You will find the following publications helpful from different points of view.

British Vocational Qualifications, London: Kogan Page, 1995.
Annual directory which, among other things, includes all essential addresses and available NVQs.

Implementing standards of competence: practical strategies for industry, Chris Lloyd and Amanda Cook, London: Kogan Page, 1993.
Aimed at the employer rather than the candidate.

Portfolio development towards national standards: a guide for candidates/ advisers and assessors, Janice Marshall, Development Processes (Publications) Ltd, 1993.
Obtainable from Development Processes (Publications) Ltd, The Granary, 50 Barton Road, Worsley, Manchester, M28 4PB.

Skillscan series, London: Pitman. Published on behalf of NCVQ. Series covers most popular NVQs.

Tax relief for vocational training, Inland Revenue, Personal taxpayer series IRI 19.
Available from your local tax office.

ABBREVIATIONS AND JARGON

Abbreviations

APA	Accreditation of prior achievement
APL	Accreditation of prior learning
ITO	Industry Training Organization
LB	Lead Body
LEC	Local Enterprise Council
NCVQ	National Council for Vocational Qualifications
NVQ	National Vocational Qualification
Scotvec	Scottish Vocational Education Council
SVQ	Scottish Vocational Qualification
TEC	Training and Enterprise Council
UKU	Underpinning Knowledge and Understanding

Jargon

Accreditation of prior achievement (APA) The assessment and accreditation of existing skills, knowledge and achievements

Accreditation of prior learning (APL) The assessment and accreditation of existing learning, including skills, knowledge and achievements

Assessor Person appointed to carry out judgement of candidate's evidence of competence

Assessment centre Organization, rather than physical location, through which assessment is carried out

Awarding body Organization appointed by Lead Body and approved by NCVQ to offer qualifications

Competence The proven ability to work to the national standard for your work

Current (1) Up-to-date; (2) Even if you acquired the skill some time ago, you still possess it

Element Smallest meaningful activity

Evidence Proof (as in a court of law) of competence

Industry Training Organization (ITO) Organization approved as representative of an industrial sector (such as gas or local govern-

ment) to promote and encourage all aspects of training. May also
function as a Lead Body

Lead Body   Organization, representative of an occupational sector
(such as design or management or the leather industry) set up by
the Department for Education and Employment to *lead the way* in
developing occupational standards and NVQs

Level   Degree of difficulty

Local Enterprise Council (LEC)   Same role, in Scotland, as Training
and Enterprise Council (TEC) in England and Wales

National Council for Vocational Qualifications (NCVQ)   Body that
establishes all requirements and oversees NVQs. Covers England,
Wales and Northern Ireland

National Vocational Qualification (NVQ)   Competence based qualification focused on the workplace

Open access   Without, as far as possible, barriers for potential candidates

Outcome   Result

Performance Criteria   Outcomes required against which candidate's
evidence will be assessed

Range   Contexts in which activity must be carried out to prove competence

Scottish Vocational Education Council (Scotvec)   Scottish equivalent
of NCVQ. Has same responsibilities in Scotland for SVQs and has
the additional role of an awarding body

Scottish Vocational Qualification (SVQ)   Scottish version of the
NVQ. Developed from same standards

Standards   The entire collection of units and elements developed for
the preparation of NVQs in a particular occupational area

Training and Enterprise Council (TEC)   Regional organization responsible, amongst other things, for promotion of training and
NVQs

Transferable   May be applied in circumstances additional to those in
which assessed

Underpinning knowledge and understanding (UKU)   The theory,
principles and understanding essential to competent performance
of NVQ units. Sometimes these need assessment additional to the
evidence from performance – testing formally or informally

Unit   A group of elements which together comprise a recognizable
function. The smallest grouping certificated

Verifier   (1) Internal verifier oversees and supports assessor and will
often coordinate programme; (2) External verifier is sent from
awarding body to oversee and advise assessment centre

WHICH NVQ IS FOR YOU?

This list gives you some idea of the NVQs you can take; but bear in mind, for example, the single heading 'Construction' includes not only 'Demolition', but most of the building trades.

Accounting
Administration
Advice, guidance, counselling and
    psychotherapy
Agricultural and garden machinery
Agricultural cooperatives
Agricultural supply
Agriculture and commercial
    horticulture
Air transport
Animal care
Arts and entertainment
Atomic energy
Bakery
Banking
Biscuit, cake, chocolate and
    confectionary
Book publishing
Bookselling
Broadcasting and film
Brush manufacture
Builders merchandising
Building management
Building products
Building services
Building societies
Bus and coach driving
Caravan industry
Care
Carpet manufacture
Cement
Ceramics
Chemical industries
Chimney sweeping
China and ball clay industries
Civil engineering
Civil service
Cleaning

Clothing industries
Coal
Commerce
Concrete
Construction
Cosmetics
Craft
Customer service
Dairy trade
Design
Distilling
Distribution
Drinks
Electrical installation
Electrical and electronics servicing
Electricity
Electronic office systems
Engineering construction
Engineering
Engineering manufacture
Engineering services
Environmental conservation
Estate agency
Extractive industries
Fabric care
Fencing
Fibre cement manufacture
Fibreboard packaging industry
Financial services
Fire emergency services
Fire industry
Food and drink industry
Footwear manufacture
Forensic science
Forestry
Frozen food industry
Furniture
Game keeping and fish husbandry

Gas

Glass

Hairdressing

Health and beauty

Health and safety

Health service

Horse care and management

Horticulture

Hotel and catering

Housing

Information and library services

Information technology

Insulation

Insurance

International trade

Jewellery

Knitting, lace and narrow fabric

Landscaping

Languages

Law

Leather

Leather goods

Lift truck operation

Management

Man-made fibres

Marine industries

Marine engineering

Marketing

Meat

Mechanical engineering

Merchant navy

Milling

Motor industry

Museums

Newspapers

Nuclear fuels

Packaging

Paint making

Paper and board industries

Paper merchandizing

Pensions

Periodicals

Personnel

Pest control

Petroleum industry

Pharmaceutical industry

Photography

Plumbing

Police

Polymer industry

Ports

Post office

Printing

Prison services

Purchasing and supply

Quarry industry

Rail

Refractories

Refrigeration

Retailing

Road haulage and distribution

Saddlery

Sales

Sawmilling

Science, technology and mathematics

Screen printing

Sea fishing

Security

Shoe repair

Sign writing

Silica and moulding sands industry

Small firms

Soap and detergent industry

Sports surfacing

Sports and recreation

Steel

Taxi services

Telecommunications

Textiles

Theatre technology

Timber

Timber merchandising

Tobacco industry

Training and development

Travel services

Veterinary surgery and nursing

Wallcovering

Warehousing

Waste management

Water industries

Waterways

Wool industry

INDEX

If you cannot find what you want in the index, try looking at the summaries at
the start of each chapter.

If you cannot find what you want in the index, try looking at the summaries at
the start of each chapter.